legacy

Martin Sharp

For
Dorothy, William and Beatrice
and
my family
Susan, Archie and Evie

All photographs courtesy of Dartington Hall Trust Archive and Sothebys.

Cover design by Robina Newman.

British Library Cataloguing-in-Publication Data.
A catalogue record for this book is available from the British Library.

ISBN 978-0-9559006-8-6

Published by Pomegranate Press, Dolphin House, St Nicholas Lane,
Lewes, Sussex BN7 2JZ
telephone: 01273 470100
email: pomegranatepress@aol.com
website: www.pomegranate-press.co.uk

Printed by Ashford Colour Press, Gosport, Hampshire PO13 0FW

Contents

Production

Legacy was first performed at the Barn Theatre, Dartington Hall, on May 15th and 16th, 2009.

Dorothy	Kathryn Pogson
Biographer and other characters	Kyle Riley
Director	Maria Pattinson
Designer	Beth Hannant
Lighting	Shaun Weager
Sound	Dave Austin
Producer	Jenny Campbell

Left to right: Michael Straight, Dorothy Elmhirst, Leonard Elmhirst, William Elmhirst. (Harbour Island, Bahamas 1959)

Introduction

The idea for this play emerged gradually from my deep interest in the work of Russian actor/theorist Mikhail Chekhov, or, as he has become known in the west, Michael Chekhov. I was curious about the belief systems and theatrical ideas/techniques that underpinned his work, and that curiosity led me towards the history of Dartington Hall.

Dorothy Elmhirst's daughter Beatrice Straight arranged for Chekhov to establish a studio at Dartington, and I made a film some years ago (*Michael Chekhov: The Dartington Years*) about Chekhov's time at Dartington Hall (1936–1938). During the making of that film, I became increasingly curious about Dorothy and Dartington Hall, and the extraordinary vision held by her and Leonard Elmhirst. The desire to create an alternative social and cultural model started as an experiment and a strong belief in new forms of education. To some it seemed utopian, but for Dorothy and Leonard it was always to be connected to the practical realities of living.

The arts, however, were to be a crucial element in practical creative living. Dorothy, encouraged by her daughter Beatrice, studied Michael Chekhov's approach to actor training, and was perhaps her personal experiment in artistic practice encouraged by her great love of literature and poetry.

I became engaged, not just in the details of Dorothy's life, but in the idea that human legacies create our heritage, and that this inheritance is absorbed and expressed as culture, as history, as language, as beliefs, as ethics and aesthetics and even as the idea of logic itself.

In this sense, we are all co-authors of our future, our present and our history – our lives become a contribution, conscious or otherwise, towards the totality of social, cultural, economic, psychological, environmental, ethical and artistic values etc. These attributes are received and perpetuated by us all. This human effect is our legacy to future generations, both individually and collectively, and for this we must accept responsibility.

Dorothy's legacy is significant, not simply through her own authentic life choices, but also through the countless lives she directly and indirectly influenced, and their subsequent contributions. Although one might argue that Dorothy's contributions were often financial, she has few equals who used their wealth in such creative and benign ways. So many initiatives, including artistic, social and political contributions, would not have found form in such positive terms without her support.

Undoubtedly Dorothy's American political expression took the form of social activism, with democratic campaigning through the influential journal, *The New Republic*. In England she moved beyond the realm of theoretical ideologies to new ways of lived experience, and for this stage Dartington Hall was created as a social experiment in natural, idealised and practical living.

When describing the play, I have often found myself using the terms 'the life and spirit of Dorothy Whitney Elmhirst'. It has seemed relevant to use these words, as a spiritual dimension to life very much absorbed Dorothy's life-long interest. She met some of the most scientific minds in the twentieth century, such as Einstein and Bertrand Russell, as well as great spiritual believers and teachers such as Rabindranath Tagore, Mahatma Gandhi and Gerald Heard.

However, Dorothy's beliefs were not to be understood as traditionally Christian. Her enquiring mind went beyond any orthodoxy, and investigated psychology and social theory as well the spiritual traditions of other cultures in order to understand her own sense of spirituality.

So who was Dorothy Payne Whitney, who became Dorothy Whitney Straight and fulfilled her destiny as Dorothy Whitney Elmhirst? Perhaps this play will shed a poetic light on a rare and exceptional woman for you to consider in her own terms and often through her own language.

Every play usually has a variety of practical inspirations and various drafts that work towards its culmination in production. I owe most to the inspiration and support of William Elmhirst, who has encouraged me in writing this play with the greatest of freedom. His trust, knowledge and generosity of spirit has been deeply moving throughout my journey in researching and developing this work.

I am also grateful to the Hermes Trust and the Arts Council England for their financial assistance and to the Dartington Hall Trust for allowing access to the Dartington Hall Archives. I am similarly indebted to Cornell University who have sent me archival material and to Sothebys for the use of Cecil Beaton's photograph. Other people who have offered advice and stories of Dorothy include Mary-Bride Nicholson, Angie St John Palmer, Yvonne Widger, Jane Brown, Mary Bartlett, Dr Rachel Harrison-French, Terry Underhill, Paul Rogers, Jennifer Lambe, Peter Cox and Karolyn Gould.

A great artistic debt is particularly owed to Kathryn Pogson, Jonathan Cullen and Maria Pattinson who with patience, trust, humour and intelligence supported me through various drafts of the play – it would be a far lesser work without their exceptional talents and creative guidance.

I am also grateful and indebted to Jenny Campbell, whose production expertise, personal encouragement and practical advice made the production tour a reality.

Lastly I am indebted to my family who have tolerated my obsession during the last few years with love.

Martin Sharp
April, 2009

Dartington's Shadow

It is perhaps hard for us to imagine the early days at Dartington when in 1925 England was recovering from the devastating effects of the First World War – the loss of her best sons in the fighting and the shattering results of this on the economy and the aristocratic social structures in the countryside especially. My father Leonard Elmhirst, although not of this background, was raised on an estate in Yorkshire owned by his father, himself the vicar of his parish. He loved to walk round the estate visiting the tenants and listening to his father discussing the problems they were facing, as their landlord and as their vicar.

My mother Dorothy, on the other hand, was an heiress at 17, when her father died. Her father William C. Whitney was a politician, a lover of the arts and one of the first conservationists. To my mother, throughout her life, the arts were essential to her sense of well being. Her motivation was to share her wealth in such a way that others could benefit as she had done from a close involvement with the arts. She was also of a deeply spiritual inclination.

After her first husband Willard Straight died, she met my father Leonard Elmhirst, who was studying at Cornell University and later sharing his agricultural knowledge with social reform projects in India. Under Rabindranath Tagore's inspiring influence, my father learned how to work with the villagers to try and stem the decline of their culture – economically, socially and artistically.

In contrast in New York, where my mother grew up, she learned how to involve herself with the problems of society in the broadest way, especially on the educational needs of the city. She took courses under John Dewey, the great pioneer of the time in education. She also took on a leadership role in many other charitable activities and was known too as a radical, supporting trade unions and the suffragettes. I believe she and my father's international influence has still yet to be truly assessed.

My parents debated whether to start their experiment in the USA or in England and finally my mother decided on England. Tagore told my father to look for somewhere in Devon, which he had visited as a young man. He then went on a search for possible properties, and when he saw the Dartington Estate he knew that he need look no further. It was in a landscape of breadth and beauty and had the one quality that he hoped to find, but was most doubtful that he could: historical associations. This historical connection went back to the Plantagenets, for King Richard II had given the property to his half brother John Holand. I subsequently discovered that my mother could trace her ancestry back to John Holand through the Whitney line, too.

I remember as a child in those early years in Dartington that there were workmen everywhere; it was not a restful environment for an excessively shy little fellow like myself. But there was a nursery community on the top floor of the Hall, where we lived apart from most of the turmoil going on around us. The Hall itself was an amazing household run on 'upstairs/downstairs' lines, with a continual influx of visitors from abroad or from London. Some people now think that this early period was the most creative time, for my parents were at the centre of things. Gradually they had to bring in managers and parts of the whole became fragmented. There was friction too between one department and another, but my parents were adept at juggling these and in keeping alive the spirit of adventure that was behind everything they were involved in.

Dartington Hall and its advent as a world-renowned centre of rural reconstruction and centre for the arts is undoubtedly a significant cultural legacy. However, a shadow has been cast across its landscape and it is my hope that I can shed some light in order that the actions of my elder brother, Michael Straight, do not taint the memory of my mother. My first concern is to protect my mother's reputation.

Because of my brother's membership of the Apostles at Cambridge in the late thirties and his continuing dedication to the Soviet cause throughout the Cold War, he secretly used both the family and others at Dartington to further the very cause that stood for everything my mother opposed. I believe that Michael Straight was certainly as important to Russia as any other member of the Cambridge spy ring. And when I first read Roland Perry's biographical account of Michael Straight's involvement with the KGB (*Last of the Cold War Spies: The life of Michael Straight*, Da Capo Press 2005), I was shocked to the core.

As a younger brother, I idolised him. I always thought that he and I had a warm and mutually supportive relationship. Only in my later years, I found his surprising outbursts of anger inexplicable. I hope that one day other members of the family will find it possible to face up to Michael's treachery.

However I believe it is important that Dartington – in its current and future forms – embraces its complex and occasionally difficult history with an openness of mind, heart and spirit; and that the Dartington Hall Trust can begin to celebrate truly, and further the extraordinary contributions that many artists, great teachers and visionary leaders have made to Dartington, while remembering the originating spiritual impulse that facilitated its creation.

William Elmhirst
2009

The Arts At Dartington

from an essay by Dorothy Elmhirst

If at Dartington we aim to provide a full and balanced life, then it would seem not only important, but essential to include the arts. For the arts are directly connected with the emotions, and as human beings, compounded of emotion as we are, we need some means of expressing in a creative way the experience that comes to us through our senses.

What after all is the meaning and function of art? Like many other problems, art is subject to a very personal interpretation. I see it as a process of discovery: discovery about ourselves and discovery about life. What an exciting experience it is when, for the first time, we discover the effect of a shadow – how it changes everything around it – or when we realise the gesture of a tree, its inner movement and form; or when we ourselves are swept away by the rhythm that catches us – the rhythm of rising smoke or trees swaying in the wind or flocks of birds or the movement of clouds or whatever it happens to be. We may have looked at these things a hundred times without being really caught into some fundamental rhythm in nature; and then suddenly a moment comes of intense realisation; one becomes aware of a profound unity and harmony underlying everything else; and it is perhaps this moment of vision that one longs to express in some form of art.

Perhaps you will want to express it through dancing – through a form of movement that unites you with this larger movement in nature; perhaps music will be your form of expression – or painting, or poetry. In drama too, we are able to go out of ourselves – to extend the limits of our own small personalities; to put ourselves imaginatively into another human being, another human situation; to touch the springs of feeling that lie beneath the surface. For art is surely a process of extending ourselves, through our sensibilities and our imagination, to something we have not reached before.

Even as we feed our bodies, so do we need to feed and sustain the imagination; and one part of the process is akin to meditation, inasmuch as it involves the sharpening of perception and awareness. If we can give ourselves the time to assimilate the experience of our senses, we can then more easily relate such experience to a central core of truth within ourselves and find some means of expression for it.

If art, then, is a process of discovery about ourselves and about life, if it brings us delight and joy, then surely it follows that we should not live without it. The great artists have always been able to communicate something new; they have penetrated so deeply into an experience that they have brought back some fresh vision: some new relationship of words, or new relationships of sound in music: a deeper insight into human beings: whatever it happens to be; they have uncovered some intense reality that lies behind all the broken and dissonant life around us; they have discovered a fundamental unity that lies at the heart of things.

That is why art is so reassuring – such a source of comfort and peace. In a great work of art all the conflicts are resolved – all the diverse elements are brought together and fused. Art is always a *bringing together* – a synthesis; and that is more and more into less and less – this difficult mechanised age when we focus on the atom. We need the other process, the process of integration, that art provides. We need the great artists; but we need also to be artists in our own way – taking time really to look at things around us: to listen, to feel, to relate one thing to another – to bring some order out of the chaos around us, and to express in some form the unity and the harmony that we feel.

And that is why it seems essential at Dartington to provide opportunities to develop the life of the imagination, and to offer the means of its expression through the arts.

legacy

Dorothy – Pink Sands, Harbour Island, Bahamas.

ACT 1 – THE AMERICAN YEARS

*A sound emerges from the silence and darkness like a deep sustained
hum. It gradually transforms with sunlight as the sound of a 1950s airline
jet lands and gives way to a Bahamian beach soundscape with tropical
bird song and gentle sounds of the Ocean. The set should evoke, even
abstractly, a Bahamian beach chalet terrace. Some stylish outdoor
furniture exists together with an element of Leonard's existence – perhaps
a summer-weight jacket or spectacles are evident.*

Dorothy starts to read from a memoir she has part-written.

DOROTHY

Monday 2nd February 1959.
I rose this morning with the dawn, And watched the slow suffusion of the
light restore to earth the pattern of the whole. And in the sky, though
clouds obscured the sun, I knew that he was there far, far above. A great
cloud caught the flame and carried high the glow from far beneath. This
is the way, I thought God shows himself to us, never directly, since the
fire would be too great, but through reflection of this light in human souls
and in the whole creation of his world.
She continues to write while speaking.
At some point towards the end of one's life, the obligation comes surely
to try and sort out for one's own satisfaction, what the permanent
influences have been. Although I do sense one's life is mysterious.
She puts down the memoir.

Biographer gradually appears.

BIOGRAPHER

What does that mean: 'Never directly, since the fire would be too great'?
And this divine light is reflected in human souls. What does that mean –
God shines and reveals his nature through humanity, all humanity?
Everybody? Hitler, Mussolini, Kylie Minogue?

DOROTHY

A biography - capturing, freezing, petrifying.

BIOGRAPHER

I write stories, factual stories – mostly factual.

DOROTHY

What facts can be known – what do facts tell us about who and what we are – 'We know what we are, but not what we may be.'
Quoting Ophelia in Hamlet, Dorothy turns towards the Biographer.
What do you know of me?

BIOGRAPHER

Pretty much everything. I've read the Swanberg biography, Hirsch's work, Croly's biography on Straight, the Rauchway essays. I've researched countless journals read your diaries, your notebooks, your letters.

DOROTHY

Words, words, words – What is the matter, my lord?

BIOGRAPHER

Matter?

DOROTHY

The matter that you read. Do you really know me?

BIOGRAPHER

I've said. I know your family history, what you did, where you travelled, who you met . . . that's a life – your life, my story.

DOROTHY

Whither should I fly?
I have done no harm. But I remember now
I am in this earthly world, where, to do harm
is often laudable; to do good, sometime
accounted dangerous folly.
Lady Macduff, Shakespeare's Macbeth.

BIOGRAPHER

I know you love poetry. What was it Shelley said? 'Poetry awakens and
enlarges the mind by a thousand unapprehended combinations of
thoughts. Poetry lifts the veil from the hidden beauty of the world.'
Defense of Poetry by Percy Bysshe Shelley.

DOROTHY

Why be – why be a biographer of me?

BIOGRAPHER

I feel its important to honour you – you're almost forgotten beyond a
small circle. You're a great woman – perhaps extraordinary.

DOROTHY

I sense your standards are rather misguided – I've known some exceptional
women, but I myself am not one of them.

BIOGRAPHER

'Some are born great, some achieve greatness and some have greatness
thrust upon them!'
Biographer quotes Twelfth Night to entice Dorothy.

DOROTHY

I seek only freedom. Why would I ever want to be trapped in pages,
defined by meanings, established by strangers?

BIOGRAPHER

Why would you want to be forgotten?

DOROTHY

Devouring Time, blunt thou the lion's paws,
And make the earth devour her own sweet brood;
Pluck the keen teeth from the fierce tiger's jaws,
And burn the long-lived phoenix in her blood;
Make glad and sorry seasons as thou fleets,
And do whate'er thou wilt, swift-footed Time,

To the wide world and all her fading sweets;
But I forbid thee one most heinous crime:

BIOGRAPHER
I know this. Shakespeare sonnet number 19, one of your favourites. What
is it?

O, carve not with thy hours my love's fair brow,
Nor draw no lines there with thine antique pen;
Him in thy course untainted do allow
For beauty's pattern to succeeding men.

Then something about 'old Time'.

DOROTHY
Yet do thy worst, old Time, despite thy wrong,
My love shall in my verse ever live young.

BIOGRAPHER
I don't understand?

DOROTHY
That's why I don't need a biographer.
*A personal computer phone bleeps its self-importance. Dorothy looks
slightly bemused. An email from his daughter's childminder has come
through. Biographer types and ends with –*

BIOGRAPHER
Calpol.

DOROTHY
Calpol?

BIOGRAPHER
My daughter.

DOROTHY

Your daughter – Calpol.

BIOGRAPHER

No, her name is Lily.

DOROTHY

Pretty name.

BIOGRAPHER

Yes, yes – You had daughters too Beatrice and . . .

DOROTHY

Ruth.

BIOGRAPHER

Beatrice, I understand was . . . is a wonderful actress.

DOROTHY

She won a Tony award for her role in The Crucible six years ago.

BIOGRAPHER

That's right. Miller on Broadway in '53. Then her Oscar.

DOROTHY

Oscar?

Beatrice Straight won her Academy Award for her supporting role in the film Network, starring William Holden in 1976, which Dorothy would not have known. Dorothy looks to the ocean.

BIOGRAPHER

No, perhaps not yet. Look I need more structure here – can we just back up a bit? I don't feel we should do the children yet. You spoke earlier: 'God shines and reveals his nature through humanity'. Do you believe that?

DOROTHY

I believe what is revealed to me.

BIOGRAPHER

Yes, but God. 'God is dead.' Nietzsche said it, and I don't feel we'll recover from that idea, do you?

DOROTHY

Nietzsche was indeed a man of interesting 'ideas', but ideas are all they were.
Sensing a dead end, for the moment, he moves to another tack.

BIOGRAPHER

Ok – can we talk about your mother, Flora? My publishers will want a clear chronology and social context.
Dorothy appears oblivious to his existence. Biographer, frustrated, sarcastically quotes Shakespeare's Macbeth as if to mock Dorothy.

BIOGRAPHER

Tomorrow and tomorrow and tomorrow
Creeps in this petty pace from day to day.

Just because you have all the time in the world to strut, I don't, for god's sake! I'm just trying to get a few simple facts here. Come on, Dorothy. What was really going on for you in February '59 with this memoir?
He closes his eyes as if to summon her again.
O speak again bright angel...
Dorothy takes over the speech from Romeo and Juliet.

DOROTHY
. . . for thou art
As glorious to this night, being o'er my head
As is a winged messenger of heaven ...

BIOGRAPHER

We don't have to do this. Retreat into Shakespeare if you want to and I'll go.

DOROTHY

Is this a dagger which I see before me,
The handle toward my hand? Come, let me clutch thee.
I have thee not, and yet I see thee still.
Art thou not, fatal vision, sensible
To feeling as to sight? or art thou but
A dagger of the mind, a false creation,
Proceeding from the heat-oppressed brain?

BIOGRAPHER

'At some point towards the end of one's life, the obligation comes surely
to try and sort out for one's own satisfaction, what the permanent
influences have been.' Your words. I'm here to help you do that – or I can
go.

DOROTHY

The truth – truth is a mysterious thing. At times illuminated, at times
concealed as in Shakespeare. Let's imagine that I was prepared talk to
you: what do you want to know?

BIOGRAPHER

Ok then, good, good. Well, let's start with your early life. You might start
with your mother – your memories of Flora Payne Whitney.
*The abstract sound motif suggesting Dorothy's inner life stirring gently
emerges from the soundscape.*

DOROTHY

I had a nurse, who I called Ma Bonne. One day we went to Lakewood
and I remember – while sitting in my room on the floor – her telling me
my mother had died. 'Madame Whitney est morte, Madame Whitney est
morte.' I was perhaps six years old. The emotion is buried. I can only
recall two memories of my mother. One at Newport, when she stood
beside me at a window on a rainy Sunday – waiting for Ma Bonne to return
from church. It was very quiet, save the rain. She held me that day – briefly.
The second memory was to say goodbye. She was lying on a couch, but
she must have been very, very ill – for it was the last time I saw her.

21

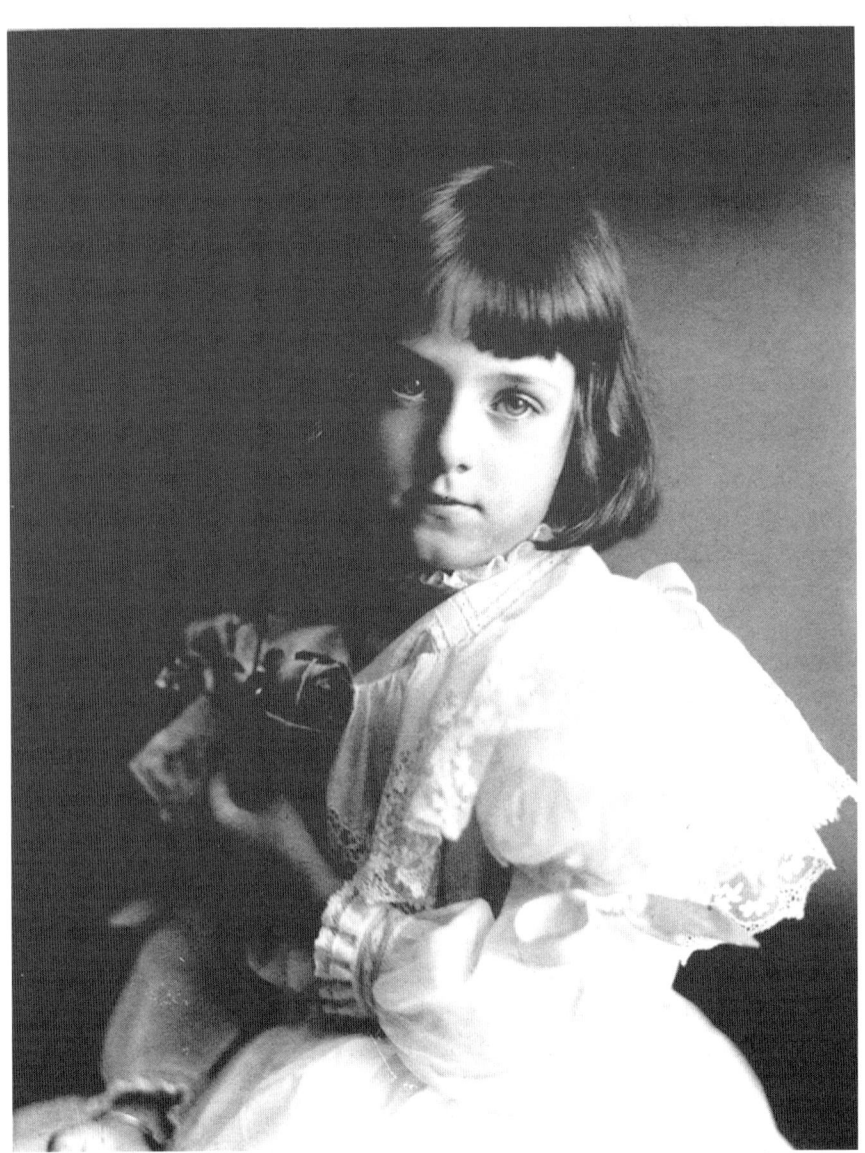

Dorothy Payne Whitney aged 8.

Tears start to flow down Dorothy's face, she surprised at her emotional response.
Perhaps the emotion isn't so deeply buried.
Dorothy summoning her positivity smiles through the tears.
The gossips said: 'Flora Payne Whitney threw extravagant parties and that her extravagance knew no bounds.' Although her exuberance was rarely very affectionate.

BIOGRAPHER
I am trying to imagine your mother – that exuberance possessing that level of wealth.

Biographer as FLORA PAYNE WHITNEY
Biographer speaks playfully with an east coast American accent.
My exuberance was boundless. Flora Payne Whitney is enigmatic and loyal. I celebrated my wealth as acts of generosity, not extravagance. Nobody every really understood that.

DOROTHY
God created an unusual destiny for my mother.

BIOGRAPHER
I imagine her as a woman slightly out of her time.

DOROTHY
And by that you're suggesting . . ?

BIOGRAPHER
That she was no shrinking violet; she knew her own mind. She didn't seek permission for her actions. I imagine her saying to your father:

Biographer as FLORA PAYNE WHITNEY
Willie, we're having a ball on Saturday, just a small one. The Morgans and Astors are coming, nothing too grand, perhaps three hundred or so. Just a small orchestra, perhaps 40. I thought we'd have a little beef with oyster to start.

DOROTHY

I remember listening in the darkness of my room to the laughter and the music of those parties. How I yearned to be an adult.

BIOGRAPHER

Children grow up too quickly. What's the Wordsworth poem? 'Shades of the prison house begin to close . . . upon the growing child.'

This is a partial line from Wordsworth's Ode Intimations of Immortality, although the Biographer gets the line slightly wrong, as the main phrase is 'Shades of the prison-house begin to close, Upon the growing Boy, But He beholds the light, and whence it flows, He sees it in his joy.'

DOROTHY

Our birth is but a sleep and a forgetting:
The Soul that rises with us, our life's Star,
Hath had elsewhere its setting,
And cometh from afar:
Not in entire forgetfulness,
And not in utter nakedness,
But trailing clouds of glory do we come
From God, who is our home:
Heaven lies about us in our infancy!

BIOGRAPHER

But all too soon lost.

DOROTHY

An innocent childhood is rare and precious.

BIOGRAPHER

Yes, indeed.
Feels the pain for Lily's severed innocence.

DOROTHY

Are you ok?

BIOGRAPHER

I'm good. Was your mother a happy woman?

DOROTHY

I sensed some tensions between her and my father.
Biographer imagines Flora's response.

Biographer as FLORA PAYNE WHITNEY

I was the happiest of all when your father gave me his entire attention,
entirely. I craved what was least available: time, blessed time. He gave
his time so freely to others. I was jealous of those 'distractions',
particularly those in pretty dresses.

DOROTHY

I remember her a little distant and always occupied.

Biographer as FLORA PAYNE WHITNEY

Oh, Willie . . .

DOROTHY

Did you want me . . .
Dorothy falters with her suspension of disbelief.

Biographer as FLORA PAYNE WHITNEY

Go on, my dear.
Dorothy breaks the spell.

DOROTHY

I can't.

BIOGRAPHER

Dorothy, she was a Payne Whitney and before that a Payne.

He smiles at his own joke.

Your mother knew she belonged to a tradition. America needed a sense of belonging, a heritage and symbols of heritage. She offered your father the opportunity to be part of that – building connections to the Vanderbilts, the Paynes, the Whitneys. Those names are symbols of pioneering Americans. Your father thought of it as developing good stock.

DOROTHY

Good stock. You're making us sound like horses.

BIOGRAPHER

The Vanderbilt, Payne and Whitney blood runs in your veins, and good stock was once considered the only important characteristic for further breeding.

DOROTHY

My parents did love each other.

BIOGRAPHER

Yes I'm sure they did, but like attracts like.

DOROTHY

I thought it was opposites. I think good feelings are not always the domain of good breeding.

BIOGRAPHER

I agree good feelings are often due to good nurturing rather than genetic inheritance, but good breeding and good nurturing have often gone hand in hand. All I'm suggesting here is that Flora was a woman of refined feelings.

DOROTHY

Yes perhaps a little too refined.

Dorothy's emotional life has been roused unexpectedly. The Biographer looks pleased.

BIOGRAPHER
Tell me more. Did you feel ignored – perhaps abused a little?

DOROTHY
Is that what you would do with my life? Analyse, trivialise, sensationalise. What are you asking of me?
I was wondering how she really felt about having children? Was it just an act of 'breeding'?

BIOGRAPHER
Your mother was undoubtedly capable of great love. I know she suffered greatly over Leonora and Olive. The letter Flora wrote to your father . . .
He reaches for a copy of the letter – Dorothy has only a vague memory.
Here it is – the letter she wrote when Olive and the boys contracted diphtheria.
La Maison De Sante, June 5th 1883.
'The only time she spoke when I could understand her was about twenty minutes before she died. Mama hold my hand rang in my ears. I went away and when I returned to see her she had on her steamer dress, a crown on her head of white rosebuds, garden pinks and white flowers at her feet with a bunch of pinks in her clasped hands.'
Dorothy reaches for the letter.

DOROTHY
'Is that my Olive lying on that white bed with candles at her head, the little face as though she must breathe, the eyes sunken, the sweet mouth and nostrils black. They all say "She is an Angel". She has her black stockings on and her little low black shoes that have danced her happy feet so often through our house.'
Why did she leave her bedside. Did she let her die alone?
Biographer reviews the letter again.

BIOGRAPHER
'I went away, and when I returned'– I'm sure there would have been a nurse.

DOROTHY

But the death of a child . . .

BIOGRAPHER

I want you to remember everything – to know who you really are.

DOROTHY

Who are you?

BIOGRAPHER

You were born on the 23rd January 1887 and christened Dorothy,
meaning gift from God, at St John's Episcopal, Washington DC. It was
in all the newspapers. President Cleveland proclaimed you the latest
addition to his cabinet. I also discovered you were born the same week as
the biggest recorded snowflake fell to earth.

DOROTHY

Really?

BIOGRAPHER

Fifteen inches wide apparently. Although, as my daughter says, surely
lots of snowflakes fall that nobody ever sees, so how do they know?

DOROTHY

She sounds a bright little girl, a challenger to the world of facts – I like
her already.

BIOGRAPHER

Lily says 'God hides in snowflakes and comes to see how beautiful the
world can be'. I suggested it seemed a cold way to travel, but she says
'God is always warm'.
Sound of mobile phone device goes off.
Connects me to the world.
Biographer lost in the world of a new email.

DOROTHY
(*Aside*)
But not the heavens I suspect.
Biographer reading an email from his publishers.

BIOGRAPHER
Interesting, very interesting.
Dorothy gasps and darts forward with joy to look at a whale offshore.

DOROTHY
Look! It's a whale! There, over there – do you see it? I didn't see one at all last year, but now already I've seen one and as close as ever. Where's Jerry with those field glasses?
Dorothy looking out towards the Ocean. The biographer, unmoved by nature, pursues his questioning.

BIOGRAPHER
Dorothy, my publisher is insisting I ask you about your son Michael's relationship with Mr Burgess. Guy Burgess, his friend from Cambridge.

Guy Burgess was an important member of the Cambridge Apostles – a self-appointed elite operating as a kind of secret debating society with various initiations and exclusive membership since 1820. Michael Straight was also an Apostle.

DOROTHY
Goodness.

BIOGRAPHER
Mrs Elmhirst?

DOROTHY
I think he'll dive under soon and we'll see that colossal fluked tail. Aren't you excited? You don't see a whale every day! It comes up to breathe for a while and then can dive for about an hour, they say. Look, there it goes – ah, such grace!

BIOGRAPHER

Yes.

DOROTHY

Quite magnificent. Jerry will be so jealous.

BIOGRAPHER

Mrs Elmhirst, might we go back to those years after your mother died.

DOROTHY

Those years are hazy.

BIOGRAPHER

Shall we sit?

DOROTHY

Mischa would say, 'Do it on your feet'. Life is movement and experience, experience the movement.

I do remember a time with Papa in the New York mansion. I remember the vast ballroom and a big dining room on the ground floor. I remember a huge staircase led to the first floor, where the main bedrooms were, and a further flight led to my playroom at the top. I also recall my brother Payne chasing me up the stairs one day, saying 'The bears are after you, the bears are after you!' I remember the excitement of feeling both safe and exposed to such dramatic danger.

BIOGRAPHER

Is that how you've experience life, as feeling both safe and exposed to danger?

DOROTHY

I have lived in the light and the dark, but increasingly I see more light.
She sees another image.
Wait, I do remember Gladys Vanderbilt. I can see it so clearly now. She lived opposite on the upper corner of Fifth Avenue and 57th. The Vanderbilt house was, to my mind, a gigantic French chateau.

Gladys and I constructed a kind of private telephone system from my bedroom right across the street to hers. I suppose it was a length of string slung across the street with cans. I used to go once a week to a dancing class there. Spanish dancing we called it. We loved dressing up for that class. Do you dance?

BIOGRAPHER
Biographer sees an another opening to be playful with Dorothy.
Actually, I love dancing! Ladies and gentlemen, I give you Gladys and Dorothy! Come Dorothy you're a trained actor – play with me. How old would you have been?

DOROTHY
Maybe ten. Gladys was about a year or so older.

Biographer as GLADYS VANDERBILT
O Dorothy, what dance are we doing tonight?
Dorothy not sure she can or wants to act.
Come on, Dorothy.
Dorothy tries to act playfully. A rumba rhythm emerges.

DOROTHY
The Rumba. What are you wearing?

Biographer as GLADYS VANDERBILT
Red of course, my red dress!

DOROTHY
Ooooh!
They dance Dorothy becoming freer with each move.

BIOGRAPHER
You look happy.

DOROTHY
I have always loved dancing. It makes me feel so free, so alive.

BIOGRAPHER

You need to dance to feel free? How could you not feel free with your wealth!

DOROTHY

(*aside*)

Is that how I will be remembered . . . a dilettante?

(*to Biographer*)

Indulge me for a while. Let's talk, but without questions.

BIOGRAPHER

But I have so many questions?

DOROTHY

Then free yourself from them – for a while at least. I remember Rudolf Laban telling me that we should dance to maintain balance. He said in ancient times priests and prophets danced for divine knowledge. To enter the mind of God, one must move.

BIOGRAPHER

The mind of God.

DOROTHY

You lack belief.

BIOGRAPHER

A sceptic perhaps. So you were close to Gladys Vanderbilt.

DOROTHY

I was close to Gladys Vanderbilt, yes.

BIOGRAPHER

Still no questions.

DOROTHY

Mischa would say, Expand, expand, expand.

BIOGRAPHER

Mischa, Michael Chekhov.

DOROTHY

Mischa would say to develop ourselves as artists we must open ourselves
up discovering more and more. Asking questions is like sifting flour. One
has already decided one wants flour without lumps; but how interesting it
might be to discover the nature of the lump?
Biographer lost the sense of the metaphor.

BIOGRAPHER

I don't quite follow –

DOROTHY

I was never good in the kitchen. Not surprising my culinary metaphors
are perhaps a trifle undercooked.
They both smile.
If you want a certain kind of answer you will ask a certain question.
Expressing oneself without questions is entirely different.
A silence commences, the Biographer lost in a world without questioning.

BIOGRAPHER

So you want me to expand, to be open?
*Dorothy amused at his inability to not ask a question, engenders an
energised frustration for the biographer.*
This will not work. I am a writer and I need information – You're my
subject!

DOROTHY

My subject.

BIOGRAPHER

Look, I'm sorry – I just meant you are the subject of this biography. I'm
obviously only interested in your history, not my own. Consider me a
fiction: no past, no future, just a man standing before a woman he wants
to understand.

DOROTHY

But you will inevitably hear things you want to hear and see things you want to see – it's your nature. Few escape the bonds of the rational mind. I will help you all I can, but I do sense my life as mysterious.

BIOGRAPHER

I write biographies. It's my job to identify key events that impact on the subject – on a person's life.

DOROTHY

So you feel all events impact on further events in someone's life – a cause will have an effect, and that effect becomes another cause, and so on.

BIOGRAPHER

Yes – well, not exactly.

DOROTHY

It sounds as if you're trying to invent a story, make me fit a plot.

BIOGRAPHER

Yes, in a manner of speaking that's what I do.

DOROTHY

But then your work discovers a life by making links across time, whereas a real life moves forward – towards destiny.

BIOGRAPHER

It's much the same thing.

DOROTHY

I beg to differ. You construct lives like a jigsaw puzzle from pieces you find. You assemble the pieces filling the spaces with appropriately shaped conjecture.

BIOGRAPHER

Have you always been this difficult?

DOROTHY

I'm not sure I follow.

BIOGRAPHER

Shall we move on.

DOROTHY

To another piece.

BIOGRAPHER

Mrs Randolph was destined to become your step-mother – a very beautiful woman by all accounts.

DOROTHY

Yes.

BIOGRAPHER

So you're maybe ten years old and your father says, 'Dorothy, my dear, I'm going to marry Edith Randolph.' And you say?

DOROTHY

I don't recall.

Biographer as WILLIAM C WHITNEY

Dorothy dear, I want us to be a family with Edith's children: Bertie and Adelaide. Edith is widowed, and since the loss of your Mama, I feel Edith is the only woman who really understands me – truly loves me – and satisfies me.

DOROTHY

I don't recognise him in your impression at all.

BIOGRAPHER

Dorothy, your father liked beautiful women. He liked intelligent women; and most of all he liked beautiful, intelligent women who liked sex. Let's face it, Dorothy, he was probably having affairs even before your mother died, even perhaps with . . .

Biographer was about to imply Mrs Edith Randolph.

DOROTHY

Why do you say such things?

BIOGRAPHER

No questions, your rules. Your mother had only been dead three years when he proposed – just a bit too soon to force a new mother on you wasn't it?

DOROTHY

Without questions.

BIOGRAPHER

Your father was a very attractive and cultured man.

DOROTHY

He was very discreet in all his relationships with women and men.

BIOGRAPHER

Men too!

DOROTHY

My father respected men and women's privacy that's all.

BIOGRAPHER

I'm damn sure many of your father's affairs were private.

DOROTHY

My father was liked by many people – perhaps envied by a few.

BIOGRAPHER

Especially after inheriting your mother's fortune.

DOROTHY

I'm not quite sure you've a point to make, but your tone sounds hostile and cynical.

BIOGRAPHER

He was a trader Dorothy, a dealer. He liked power and he saw the route to it paved with gold.

DOROTHY

What evidence do you have for this?

BIOGRAPHER

Now it seems you have real questions. The ethics involved in financing the New York Metropolitan Railway appear seriously questionable. Many investors lost thousands of dollars. Swanberg says . . .

DOROTHY

You see, I like to believe the best in people, and the truth is often complex. My experience is that it's easier for people to simplify things for the sake of a story, rather than discover the complex truth of a matter. Shall we move on?

BIOGRAPHER

I thought we were exploring a lump. A flour lump, or was it perhaps too sticky.

DOROTHY

This is your story not mine, and not my fathers'.

BIOGRAPHER

Your Uncle, one of the richest men in New York. He vowed to disinherit any of you who went against his will and supported your father in marrying Edith. So your father offered you the choice between living with him or your Uncle yes?

DOROTHY
My father wanted us to be free in our choices.

BIOGRAPHER
But it makes no sense. Your Uncle Oliver and your father were best
friends at Yale. Why would your Uncle be so destructive to the family?

DOROTHY
Loyalty is a very powerful thing. I think my Uncle felt his sister's
memory would be betrayed if my father re-married – but many things in
life are unknowable.
Biographer is frustrated by the lack of conclusion. He wants his world
black and white, a world of facts. She offers him a fact.
I did feel my father deserved to be happy.
Satisfied for the moment, he seeks another piece of his puzzle.

BIOGRAPHER
Some people think your father was having an affair with Mrs Randolph
before your mother died.

DOROTHY
What actually are you trying to discover here?

BIOGRAPHER
The facts, just the facts.
He takes up her memoir.
You've written here: 'Mrs Edith Randolph, my new stepmother, was very
good to me and I loved her dearly. She was the first person I can remember
who ever kissed me good night.'

DOROTHY
That's true.

BIOGRAPHER
And then the accident happened.

Young Dorothy.

DOROTHY

Is this important to your story?

BIOGRAPHER

Is it important to yours?
She acknowledges the point and takes the memoir.

DOROTHY

A terrible thing happened one day. I was riding immediately behind my stepmother. Mrs Randolph was on a magnificent horse. It was a glorious day and we were all riding so well. I was fast approaching my stepmother, but we were heading toward a low bridge with an overhanging construction. She must have failed to see it, you see, for suddenly I realised she had been struck by it and fallen off her horse.

BIOGRAPHER

Actually that's not quite the version of events I've researched. My notes suggest she was riding a new horse, a bigger horse. I think she misjudged the obstacle.

DOROTHY

What difference does that make now! Edith broke her back and was paralysed, and you're curious about whether it was her fault or not!

BIOGRAPHER

You're right. I'm sorry.

DOROTHY

It was devastating for my father.

BIOGRAPHER

I've no doubt.

DOROTHY

I remember he studied medical journals long into the night.

BIOGRAPHER

Biographer reveals his own deep anger and frustration with the medical profession and identifies with William C Whitney's desire to find his own answers.

The medical profession is full of charlatans who know nothing! They knew nothing in the last century, they know nothing in this and will no doubt learn precious little in the next!

DOROTHY

You did that very well. Papa was often very angry about Edith's situation. It was a tragic and mysterious event.

BIOGRAPHER

There is nothing mysterious about spinal injury or disease – just lack of knowledge!

DOROTHY

One day Edith asked me to stand by her bedside. She was in such terrible pain, but she wanted to tell me the facts of life – about menstruation and the shock it might cause me. At this last and tragic moment, she was thinking of me; of how to help me face the future.

BIOGRAPHER

I understand she sustained her passion for horses, and shortly after watching the Meadow Brook steeplechase fell into a coma and died on May 6th, 1899.

DOROTHY

She was only forty one years old. She had brought such gaiety to Papa and me.

BIOGRAPHER

So many lives change in such tragedies.

DOROTHY

I see her now always surrounded by light.

BIOGRAPHER
You loved her very much, didn't you?

DOROTHY
Enough now, please.
The Biographer feels the parallel between Dorothy's loss and his daughter Lily.

BIOGRAPHER
Fathers and daughters form strong attachments. My daughter Lily gives me great strength.

DOROTHY
You have a sadness around you – have you lost someone close?

BIOGRAPHER
We haven't spoken about your sons.

DOROTHY
No.

BIOGRAPHER
May we do that?

DOROTHY
Whitney was like my father. So much of that little baby boy was him – so headstrong, so determined.

BIOGRAPHER
He was a pilot at sixteen with a real licence?

DOROTHY
Yes.

BIOGRAPHER

And he raced cars and . . . has developed an astonishingly successful career in the aircraft industry.
The pause in the line suggests the Biographer is now cautious about using the present rather than past tense.

DOROTHY

An engineering heart and a business brain. You've researched Whitney too?

BIOGRAPHER

A little. And Michael and William?

DOROTHY

Well, they're both here. Would you like to meet them?

BIOGRAPHER

They're here?

DOROTHY

We've been coming here every year since '55 – since I was first ill.

BIOGRAPHER

Since your heart attacks.

DOROTHY

Yes. Michael is here with his wife and their children, and my youngest son Bill has come over for a holiday, too. Perhaps they might join us. Michael is a writer, too, and William an actor.
Dorothy moves away from him momentarily as he calls out towards her.

BIOGRAPHER

You're a highly influential transatlantic figure – a social activist and arts patron. Mrs Elmhirst, you're as closed as hell. How do I get through? Whales, Shakespeare, Bahamas . . .

BIOGRAPHER

You wonder what a biographer will make of your life, Dorothy! I tell you – goddamned privileged! Jesus.

I'm the writer – I've created icons and destroyed heroes. You – what have you ever created? What did you make happen that didn't need a big fat cheque book! And you try to censor my questions – questions that seek only for some truth, Dorothy! What have you ever lost, really lost? *Dorothy muses on his attack and his pain.*

DOROTHY

I lost papa . . .

BIOGRAPHER

What?

DOROTHY

I lost papa when I was seventeen. He was taken ill during Parsifal at the Metropolitan Opera and carried home. Papa was in pain for about five days before he allowed the appendectomy.

BIOGRAPHER

Yes, your father – and he died during the operation, didn't he.

DOROTHY

Yes.

BIOGRAPHER

I understand you collapsed at the Woodlawn Cemetery.

DOROTHY

Yes . . . yes, I remember that now.

BIOGRAPHER

So both parents lost and an orphan at seventeen.

DOROTHY

Yes. My brother Harry was appointed my guardian and executor.

BIOGRAPHER

But later you received seven million dollars – all very well invested, I believe, making a very substantial fortune and you a very eligible heiress.

DOROTHY

Eligible for a society match, although not so eligible emotionally perhaps. Can you understand that?

BIOGRAPHER

Yes. I'm really sorry. I feel I owe you an apology.

DOROTHY

There is no need. I understand, you see – we share the same world. I found purpose in life through the Junior League, if not meaning.

Biographer as JUNIOR LEAGUER

Biographer mimics a zealous Junior Leaguer.
We must prove that we are very good girls, that all the money and time which has been spent on us is not a lost investment to the world, that we are worth something in life.

DOROTHY

Does it appear such a strange idea to you?

BIOGRAPHER

It can be seen as a legitimation for wealth.

DOROTHY

What would you have me do – lock myself away? Give away every dollar to charities? I accepted the responsibilities that went with wealth, but followed my own path.
Dorothy made significant contributions and investments into many social causes, including the trade unions and the suffragettes.

BIOGRAPHER
(*sarcastically*)
You did travel extensively too.

DOROTHY
So judgemental. My travels have been a spiritual journey. St Marks in
Venice and images from Chartres will always be with me. The incense,
the music, the liturgy. All so evocative and drawing me upwards, always
inexorably upwards.

BIOGRAPHER
I visited Chartres Cathedral. I remember a little old woman in a floral
housecoat operating a deafening vacuum cleaner by the altar. There was
something profoundly incongruous – the serenity broken by such a
cacophony.

DOROTHY
The kingdom of heaven is within us all.

BIOGRAPHER
Do you really believe what you said, that 'God shows himself through
reflections?'

DOROTHY
Yes, I do.

BIOGRAPHER
As a biographer I'm obviously curious about people's lives and the
principles that form them. Do you recognise yourself in this diary?
Biographer passes her a tiny gold leaf diary.

DOROTHY
'When the right person comes along, I wonder if one has any doubts,
even then.' This is my travel diary? 'I can't help longing for certain
things. He must be strong and he must be tender. He must be honest and
generous and kind and thoughtful. I don't think I could fall in love with a

man who had no ambition and no aim in life, because I feel a great longing to be part of his work. And then, besides, if he lacked ambition I could not admire him.'

BIOGRAPHER
Perhaps a romantic novel too many?

DOROTHY
This is my diary – how have you come by this?

BIOGRAPHER
We'll come to that. Can we talk about your meeting with Willard?

DOROTHY
It was expected that I would marry well and had many suitors. I wanted to marry, but felt I was demanding too much, though I now know that some guiding spirit was right in withholding consent– waiting for a man I could really love.

BIOGRAPHER
Willard.

DOROTHY
I went to China and was met by Willard in Peking. He took us back to one of the Embassy houses . . .

BIOGRAPHER
And when you first met, what did you feel?

DOROTHY
That he was very handsome. Very capable. A very impressive man.

BIOGRAPHER
A man you could love?

Dorothy and Willard (far right) in China.

DOROTHY

For a fortnight I lived in a magical world. Each day visiting temples or riding out to the plains. Willard was a brilliant Chinese scholar. He made every contact easy. One day we set off to the Ming Tombs, a long and exciting journey, and on that day I realised I'd found the man I could love.

Biographer initially plays Willard as a gauche New Yorker

Biographer as WILLARD

Dorothy, Dorothy will you be mine? I hold no store by your seven million dollars at all!

DOROTHY

If you're not going to be serious.

Biographer as WILLARD

His mood and accent changes: Willard the sensitive artist and diplomat surfaces.

Miss Whitney, my heart is as China, vast and deep.

DOROTHY

Then let China be assured that no political unrest or economic situation could disturb her.

Biographer as WILLARD

But I will be so alone in my China without you.

DOROTHY

Your China will not be destroyed. You must keep it safe and help it grow strong.

Biographer as WILLARD

Miss Whitney!

DOROTHY

Dorothy, Dorothy.
Breaking the suspension of disbelief.
We knew we must be patient.

BIOGRAPHER

You were patient lovers, then?
Dorothy offers an accusatory stare.
Yes, of course. Kindred souls, fellow orphans and passionate idealists.
The only real difference, Willard was the son of a school teacher, and you
– you were a Payne Whitney, a multi-million dollar heiress.

DOROTHY

I like to think we were equals in slightly different circumstances.

BIOGRAPHER

You married in September 1911 after resolving the resistance from your
family to the alliance.

DOROTHY

We returned to China, but within six months the Chinese Revolution led
by Sun Yat Sen forced us back to New York – otherwise we would have
stayed.

BIOGRAPHER

I understood you virtually fled under gunfire.

DOROTHY

The rebels were quite close, yes.

BIOGRAPHER

And you were pregnant.

DOROTHY

We returned to New York and built a home. Whitney was born in
November 1912. Then we had Beatrice and Michael.

BIOGRAPHER
And the New Republic and Asia journals were further fruits of your union.

DOROTHY
We were inspired to bring new ideas and knowledge to America.

BIOGRAPHER
I sense he was attracted to the exotic. I imagine Willard thinking the New York commercial world quite aggressive and perhaps unethical.
With a deep sincerity - an artist's soul in the body of a diplomat. His voice has a slow deliberating tempo.

Biographer as WILLARD
To me, New York is just a commercial bar room brawl, where men trade stocks rather than punches. This is the world, Dorothy, of your father, of the William C. Whitneys, not me, not Willard Straight.

DOROTHY
Your voice is wrong, but the sentiment is possibly true.

BIOGRAPHER
Then the First World War started and Willard went to Paris to set up insurance provision for American soldiers – and then came the news from Paris.

DOROTHY
Yes.

BIOGRAPHER
I have actual copies of those telegrams from the Cornell archives.

DOROTHY
I'm not sure if . . .

BIOGRAPHER
The first Western Union cable from Paris. It's dated November 25th,
1918. 'Willard Straight has influenza pneumonia at Crillon Hotel – stop –
is in care of General Thayer and best American physicians here – stop –
condition serious, but hopeful – stop.' It was followed a day later by
further details from your dear friend Daisy Harriman: 'Willard's
temperature 102 and eight-tenths, pulse 104, respiration 24.' Five days
later, you received – this cable from Daisy Harriman.
Biographer hands her the final cable.

DOROTHY
Willard passed away peacefully at 12:45am December 1st – stop.
I delivered all your messages to him – stop. His last request was that I
should cable you his love – stop. All your and Willard's friends here were
near him at the last and through it all their thoughts and love have been
with you – stop, stop, stop.
She raises a hand to stop him speaking again as the stage is split by light.
The Biographer in his own isolated world of biographical creation muses.

BIOGRAPHER
Stop – yes, stop. Perhaps I should add – No, I'll stop here for the
moment. I should ring Cathy to see if Lily is ok.
He picks up his phone and goes to call his childminder Cathy. Dorothy
drawn closer towards the Ocean.

DOROTHY
You left me, sweet, two legacies,
A legacy of love
A Heavenly Father would content,
Had He the offer of;
You left me boundaries of pain
Capacious as the sea,
Between eternity and time,
Your consciousness and me.
The Emily Dickinson poem gives rise to a dramatic expression of anguish
as this moment bleeds into darkness and emptiness.

ACT II – THE ENGLISH EXPERIMENT

Dorothy closes her eyes and appears summoned – she stretches wide her arms, suggesting a circle – the soundscape (perhaps a choral or abstract sound) evokes a strong atmosphere.

DOROTHY
We formed a circle like this around a table. Mary K had some fruit – apples and plums, I think, and a jug of water on a large round walnut table. I remember a strong scent and an odd atmosphere in the room. The lights were low – just a few candles.
A silence falls as Dorothy incorporates the image.

BIOGRAPHER
You asked the medium.
Dorothy absorbed in the memory. The biographer speaks slightly louder.
You asked the medium what, exactly?

DOROTHY
It felt very strange at first, but I asked about our children. Mary K suggested Whitney would have a very successful business career.

BIOGRAPHER
And Beatrice?

DOROTHY
Beatrice she said would become a great artist, although it was suggested she would be a challenging child – and she was. Oh, what an extraordinary spirit Beatrice has become!

BIOGRAPHER
My daughter Lily is a challenging little girl. She reminds me – of her mother.

DOROTHY

Are you divorced?

BIOGRAPHER

Why do you say that?

DOROTHY

I see 'alone-ness' surrounding you.

BIOGRAPHER

We weren't married, she – she was my partner.

DOROTHY

I see. Losing her . . .
The biographer stops her interrogation.

BIOGRAPHER

Losing Willard must have been very painful for you.
Dorothy accepts his deflection.

DOROTHY

Twenty million people died in that flu pandemic. What a terrible fate – all
those families affected by the vastness of loss. Some say that great flood
of souls passing over created a winter tide in the spirit world. I sense the
ebb and flow of that tide still. I don't want to shut out or obliterate the
war from my mind. It is always with me in one way or another, but I want
to find some truth, some faith, that can redeem the war; and yet the
answer doesn't come. So you see, although I do face it, I haven't
overcome it.
Dorothy refers to the 'great flu' of 1918–19.

BIOGRAPHER

How did you cope though?

DOROTHY

I'm not sure I did cope. I had the children – and belief – and poetry. Poetry creates a presence for me beyond this world. That time after Willard I was lost. My wanderings now, though, seem as eternal.

BIOGRAPHER

It obviously shook your faith . . .

DOROTHY

Actually it was a renewal of faith. I had understood faith in a very simple way. It became a more complex and subtle quality after Willard passed.

BIOGRAPHER

You commissioned a biography of Willard from the *New Republic* editor Herbert Croly. That was your way to immortalise him! That is the power of biography – the deepest significance in the face of the existential void is literature.

Dorothy muses on the deeper question, but deflects her motivation for Willard's biography as a means to immortalise his memory.

DOROTHY

I did not seek immortality for Willard in a book. The biography was just a way to record his work, not his life.

BIOGRAPHER

How can I convince you biographies are important? That's what I want for you and your family – a record. I'm sure a biography will be a written about your son Michael as well. What did Mary K say about him?

DOROTHY

That he would be complex, literary and deep minded.

BIOGRAPHER

Her predictions appear to have been very accurate.

DOROTHY

Or Willard's.

BIOGRAPHER

Yes I see – you see them as Willard's predictions. Although you never turned to mediums again.

DOROTHY

No – I have developed my own spiritual relationship with Willard.

BIOGRAPHER

I have a question for you. It seems difficult to ask as it concerns the reputation of your son Michael.

DOROTHY

Why now so diffident?

BIOGRAPHER

People have suggested Michael was involved with the KGB, and I wondered if you knew . . .

DOROTHY

What a strange thing to say.

BIOGRAPHER

It's difficult to explain. Things may – will, I'm sure – come out in the fullness of time. Is it at all conceivable to you that Michael has worked for the KGB?

DOROTHY

I think your research has lead you on a fool's errand. Mike, you see, studied economics at Cambridge and became friendly with the Apostle group – not quite sure what distinguished them.

BIOGRAPHER

He knew Guy Burgess, though.

DOROTHY

Yes, he did actually, and Mike was very shocked and upset when he defected.

BIOGRAPHER

May 25th '51 with Donald Maclean.

DOROTHY

Goodness, you do like your facts, don't you? Mr Burgess came to our home in England in the '30s. He rather enjoyed drinking as I recall, and – cricket, I remember – he liked cricket.

BIOGRAPHER

Yes he liked his boy's games.
Biographer alludes to the homosexual promiscuity for which Guy Burgess was quite renowned.

DOROTHY

I have to be honest – I didn't really care for Guy Burgess. He was undoubtedly a very intelligent young man, and I think Michael was slightly in awe of him, but to my mind, rather crude.

BIOGRAPHER

Dorothy, I think Michael has a historical connection with the KGB which some have considered an extensive involvement.
The Biographer is alluding to Roland Perry's book, Last of the Cold War Spies: The life of Michael Straight, published in 2005.

DOROTHY

We must call him down. He would find this all very funny.

BIOGRAPHER

All the *right* thinking Cambridge students were *left* thinking.

DOROTHY

You should use that. He is around somewhere working on a book.

BIOGRAPHER

I know some of his fictional work. I would be interested to talk to him. You seem very proud of your children?

DOROTHY

Children expose who we really are and inform many of the life choices we make. After Willard passed I began to understand where I stood, where I belonged and what I believed in – the importance of the individual, the right of free speech and a free press. The redistribution of wealth, democratic institutions, tolerance, an interacting world brotherhood and sisterhood – these ideas gave my life purpose.

BIOGRAPHER

Though perhaps not meaning?

DOROTHY

Meaning is ours only to seek, not to find.

BIOGRAPHER

Willard's will brought you to Leonard Elmhirst. Did the medium Mary K have that foresight?

DOROTHY

She mentioned more children – a child of the earth and a child of the sky, she said. I didn't understand that at first, but they were, of course, Ruth and Bill.

BIOGRAPHER

And yet the meeting with Leonard might never have happened – you missed his appointment three times.
The biographer is almost incredulous that she fails to realise the significant consequences of their never meeting, and the subsequent futures for so many that would have been different.

DOROTHY

Twice, I think. I made the third occasion. But yes, my life might have been very different had Leonard not been persistent.
Dorothy eventually met Leonard Elmhirst at the Colony Club in New York in late summer 1920.

BIOGRAPHER

Can you remember that meeting?

DOROTHY

I was full of apology: 'I'm so sorry I'm late, Mr Elmhirst.'
Dorothy initiates the play and the Biographer quickly joins in.

Biographer as LEONARD

Mrs Straight, I quite understand you are a very busy woman of course.

DOROTHY

You need a little more of the young English squire. Busy or not, it's quite unforgivable.
Biographer refines the English accent.

Biographer as LEONARD

I'm here to discuss Cornell. Do you know the university?

DOROTHY

That's better. No, Cornell is not very familiar to me, but as you perhaps know, my late husband made a bequest in his will for Cornell.

Biographer as LEONARD

I've heard many excellent things of Major Straight. Most dreadful tragic loss to you and your country. I, I myself, lost two dear brothers.

DOROTHY

How can I help you Mr Elmhirst?

Biographer as LEONARD

Well, I'm here representing the overseas students at Cornell. There –
there is a problem with the Cosmopolitan Club. It's a very special
community – so few places where you can meet other foreigners. So
important, don't you think? Too easy to live in your own world without
understanding others?

DOROTHY

I'm sure you're quite right Mr Elmhirst. The nature of the problem?

Biographer as LEONARD

I, I, I've been appointed the President of the Cosmopolitan. Hope that's
not the problem, eh? Anyhow, it has been put to me to, er . . .

DOROTHY

The problem Mr Elmhirst?

Biographer as LEONARD

Yes – well – financially things are a little awkward.

DOROTHY

Eighty thousand dollars worth of awkwardness I understand.

BIOGRAPHER

I knew you could act, although I hear some thought you a terrible actress.

DOROTHY

I've not done anything like that since working with Mischa. I'd forgotten
how much fun it can be – terrible or not. You were good. A little too arch
English perhaps, but there was something of Leonard there. Something
very sincere about Leonard – I intuitively had great faith in him.

BIOGRAPHER

You do have considerable faith though.

DOROTHY

You make it sound a very simple thing. I have found it profoundly difficult to sustain. It has taken many forms in my life, but my relationship with Leonard became a journey based on faith – yes, and trust, of course.

BIOGRAPHER

But the Cornell bequest and the meeting with Leonard was all connected to Willard's will?

DOROTHY

It sounds very auspicious put like that. We agreed that a student union building would be built to enrich student life, and that became Willard's gift to Cornell.

BIOGRAPHER

And the dedication –
Biographer unfolds the letter.

DOROTHY

You have that too.

BIOGRAPHER

'Treat all women with chivalry. The respect of your fellows is worth more than applause. Understand and sympathise with those who are less fortunate than you are. Make up your own mind, but respect the opinion of others. Don't think a thing right or wrong because someone tells you so. Think it out yourself, guided by the advice of those whom you respect. Hold your head high and keep your mind open. You can always learn.' And that to this day is the inscription in Willard Straight Hall.

DOROTHY

May I see?
He passes her the letter.
Willard wrote this to our eldest son Whitney just before Willard left for France.
Biographer acknowledges the fact.

'Dear Whitney You may never see this letter. I hope you never will. But should anything happen to me I want you to have a word – you as the oldest – that you may have it for yourself and your blithe young sister and your brother Michael. My father died when I was seven years old, and I had no word save such as my mother gave me. She was taken, too, before I knew what she meant. I trust, for your sake all three of you, your mother will be there to guide you. All the best in you comes from her; all the finest in you will be brought out by her. You are blessed as no other children have been blessed with such a mother. Treat all women with chivalry . . . '
Dorothy, moved, passes the letter back to the biographer.

BIOGRAPHER

You ok?

DOROTHY

Yes.

BIOGRAPHER

I found a story that Leonard tells about one of your first meetings at Cornell. In Enfield Glen.

DOROTHY

Enfield Glen.

BIOGRAPHER

The biographer does not speak 'you died' – it's a psychical stumble between their two realities.
Leonard wrote it all down after . . . [you died] Here –
Biographer passes her the letter.

DOROTHY

'We had decided to take a picnic supper into Enfield Glen and having gathered a basket of food, we were dropped around 3pm at the foot of the Glen.' I remember this! 'It started to rain and poured until evening, when we were picked up again. It was from my angle a perfect picnic.' Wasn't it just! 'With the help of my old Army blanket, I rigged up a tent that kept the rain off my guest, although a good stream ran down my back. The matches of course got wet, so we had to do without corn, the steak and the coffee. She made the best comrade I've ever had and seemed to enjoy every minute of the adventure.' I did, I really did! 'I still know her less than ever, but much better than ever before.' Leonard was so resourceful, I had no doubt after that he would achieve great things in India.

BIOGRAPHER

He showered you with letters for four years and made two marriage proposals which you refused.

DOROTHY

Willard was always a presence. Leonard, or Jerry as I call him, was so young and ambitious. I didn't want to tie him to a relationship. I wanted to support him with his work in India.

BIOGRAPHER

With Tagore.
Dorothy creates the sense that Rabindranath Tagore could be manipulative.

DOROTHY

Tagore was like a father to him. I liked Tagore, but he was a very clever and ambitious man – more so after winning the nobel prize I believe.

BIOGRAPHER

You gave his projects a lot of money over the years.
Dorothy nods.

DOROTHY

I believed in Leonard and the work in India.

BIOGRAPHER

At Santiniketan.
Dorothy nods. (Santiniketan, pronounced Shantiniketôn, means place of peace.)

BIOGRAPHER

And Tagore was of course very pleased you eventually accepted
Leonard's proposal of marriage.

DOROTHY

Yes he was.
Biographer smiles.
Are you a cynical man?

BIOGRAPHER

No I don't think so.

DOROTHY

You believe Tagore was manipulative?

BIOGRAPHER

I believe there is a shadowy side to most of us.

DOROTHY

And my shadowy side?

BIOGRAPHER

Well I know you sent an attractive nurse to help at Santiniketan – perhaps
to tempt and test Leonard?

DOROTHY

So you want to reveal my shadows?

BIOGRAPHER

To be human is to be flawed, is it not? Biography readers want a sense of
the real person behind the mask. I've shown all my subjects in this way.
Public figures cultivate masks – personas I think the analysts call it.

DOROTHY

So you think I hide?

BIOGRAPHER

Look, I'm not some hack trying to dig up skeletons. I'm just interested in a little old-fashioned truth. Have you got things to hide?

DOROTHY

I cannot give good answers to questions, where reasons for some of my actions are themselves mysterious.

BIOGRAPHER

You see I think mysteries as just mental smokescreens. Mysteries are merely unfound truths awaiting discovery.

DOROTHY

You wanted to talk about Leonard?

BIOGRAPHER

Ok, let's do that. Leonard Knight Elmhirst – I love that Knight Elmhirst. Makes him sound like a Templar. Leonard is six years younger than you, of course.

DOROTHY

Is that significant for you?

BIOGRAPHER

Its always amused me how women are shy about their age. Why is that?

DOROTHY

There speaks a man! Actually, I'm not shy about my age. Age means only three things for me – that I struggle to stand after weeding the garden, that my eyesight is fading, but that my inner sight develops day by day before the mystery of death.

BIOGRAPHER

Do you love Leonard in the way you loved Willard?

DOROTHY

Originally I didn't imagine the relationship would develop romantically with Leonard.

BIOGRAPHER

But it did though?

DOROTHY

Yes, of course. Do you know Leonard?

BIOGRAPHER

Not exactly.

DOROTHY

He's around somewhere, probably looking for that yellow-throated warbler we glimpsed earlier.

BIOGRAPHER

It took a while to win your hand in marriage.

DOROTHY

I needed time.

BIOGRAPHER

His letters show him very persistent.

DOROTHY

I admire constancy. Leonard proved himself constant – not so many did.

BIOGRAPHER

That was the Knight in him, and his quest to succeed in Tagore's India. *His tone becomes softer, exploring his own dilemma regarding future relationships.*
How did the children take to him?

DOROTHY

Actually they adored him right from the start. It was Beatrice, I think, who first called him Jerry. Leonard sounded much too formal, too British perhaps. One day he became Jerry and it stuck. I think he was always a Jerry really. Leonard was the intrepid adventurer, diplomat, politician and pioneering agriculturalist; Jerry the birdspotter and raconteur. It has caused no end of confusion on occasions.

BIOGRAPHER

You really are much more spirited and fun than I thought you'd be.

DOROTHY

I'm pleased. People are seldom how they first appear – even you.

BIOGRAPHER

Can I ask you a personal question?

DOROTHY

It seems rather late to seek permission.

BIOGRAPHER

This letter before the marriage. I was curious –
You say here: 'One of these days I won't be a moody creature any longer. Experience will integrate me, more experience of you. So many couples I know are happy and therefore successful in their marriage, but they haven't grown as a result of it, and that surely is the final test. I want to lose the old Dorothy and find a new one with you.'
So you eventually felt it was ok to marry again even with the children. You saw it as a means of growth?

DOROTHY

I was guided to this. I listened to my heart and to Willard.

BIOGRAPHER

But Willard was dead.

Dorothy and Leonard, Dartington Hall, 1925.

DOROTHY

Dead as his body, but not dead for me!

BIOGRAPHER

The biographer does not really understand what Dorothy's truly believes,
so tries to test her spiritual connection to Willard.
So he approved the marriage?

DOROTHY

Yes.

BIOGRAPHER

You married Leonard in April '25 though you changed the vows – an
element of distrust?

DOROTHY

I was very happy to love and honour, but 'obey' didn't feel quite right.

BIOGRAPHER

Seems a radical thing to impose at that time.

DOROTHY

It was important to me. 'Be the change you want,' Mr Gandhi said to us.
I like that idea – be the change you want.

BIOGRAPHER

Let's play. Where exactly were you when you decided about England
and your plans with Leonard or Jerry – or whatever I should call him.

DOROTHY

I'm sure we were at the old family home in Connecticut – and I think you
should call him Leonard.

BIOGRAPHER

I'll be Leonard then. Can you imagine the scene?

DOROTHY

Ok.

BIOGRAPHER

Ok.

Dorothy poised and tight.

DOROTHY

Yes – I'm ready.

BIOGRAPHER

I was waiting for you.

DOROTHY

Oh, I think I said something like: 'Jerry I want to create a school.'
Actually it was much more serious: 'Jerry I want to create a school, let's
make a school, a place where education is a joyful discovery, part of life's
journey itself, rather than a place to impart knowledge, which is so
limiting to a child.'

Biographer as LEONARD

Of course, though we must be prepared for troubled waters and faulty
navigation.

DOROTHY

We must adopt the right attitude towards any obstacles.

Biographer as LEONARD

Let's agree there'll be no blame on the wind or compass, just new
directions and lessons learnt.

They both imagine their own versions of the experiment.

DOROTHY

O yes, yes, a glorious experiment! With artistic activities of all kinds:
Music . . .

Biographer as LEONARD
Yes of course, and we'll have poultry . . .

DOROTHY
Yes, yes . . . a few chickens in the garden. That would be lovely!

Biographer as LEONARD
Well, more a farm really, and . . .

DOROTHY
Perhaps a theatre group . . . Yes!

Biographer as LEONARD
I see it as an experiment in rural re-generation – town thinking meets
country living.

DOROTHY
Arts and crafts supporting a balanced life.

BIOGRAPHER AS LEONARD
We'll need good pasture for the cattle and sheep, a small forest for timber
and an orchard, and perhaps . . .

DOROTHY
Opera! A small operatic troupe. Yes, of course, the farm and crops and
things – but a school and the arts combined with industry and agriculture.
Oh Jerry, what fun it will be!

Biographer as LEONARD as TAGORE
'To release the imagination, to give it wings, to open wide the door of the
mind, this is perhaps the most vital service that one being can render
another'.
They have both enjoyed the moment, but break the convention.

DOROTHY

Tagore?

BIOGRAPHER

Tagore.

DOROTHY

In Devonshire.

BIOGRAPHER

How was my accent?

DOROTHY

Dorothy in a Russian accent.
It was good, but you must see the words as if streaming from your eyes.
Radiate, radiate!

BIOGRAPHER

Mischa Chekhov?

DOROTHY

Yes. I'm beginning to enjoy this. Is this how you intend to unmask me?

BIOGRAPHER

I transcribed a talk Leonard did about the Dartington purchase. He was
quite the raconteur. Let me try the accent again.
Prepares for the raconteur performance.
Schooool, Schoooll – We're going to have a schooool.

Biographer as LEONARD

So one day, one day I was in London and I walked into Messrs Knight
Frank and Rutley, Hanover Square. There was a man with an enormous
desk and I sat on the edge of a chair and he said *'Sir what can I do for
you?'* I said I want a place. *'Hunting, shooting, fishing, golf!'* No, I said,
not especially. *'How many bedrooms?'* I said, I've not the least idea, not
the least idea. Agriculture, you see, was no longer paying, and so estates

were being picked up by businessmen either for sport – hunting, shooting, fishing, golf – or for weekending out from the City. And these were the two reasons people came in to see this man.

He said '*What do you want, what do you want?*' He thought I was crackers. I said first of all it must be beautiful because we're going to have a school; and secondly it must have a good shire because we're going to make farming pay; and thirdly, variety – farmland, forest, orchard – and if you can give me those, then historical association thrown in would be splendid.

Anyhow, I had been once to Devon and I thought it was like paradise, so I said to my little sister who knew someone in the motor trade that I needed a motor car. So I said, come to London. So on the Monday we bought a car and on Tuesday we took lessons how to drive it and got a licence. No tests needed in those days of course. So on Wednesday we set off! We made Exeter that night in a highly nervous condition. And the next day we went to see Dartington Hall.

DOROTHY

When I saw the estate I was a little surprised; perhaps shocked is a better word. I was convinced roof tiles were being displaced by our very breath, and heaven knows what assaults would occur when the east wind blew. The great hall's roof was gone and the courtyard and gardens were in a sorry state. I did wonder myself if Leonard had gone a little crackers, but he had such vision you see. He could see potential, where others, like me, saw mere ruins.

BIOGRAPHER

But you agreed to buy it?

DOROTHY

As I said, my relationship with Jerry was built on faith. After we bought Dartington and committed to the experiment, I felt a strange freedom. Free from being a Whitney and all that legacy entailed, free from the lawyers and the New York accountants and free to do something creative and true to my spirit. It's perhaps hard to appreciate how detached I had become in my rather odd life with its extremes of wealth and privilege.

Wealth often separated me from everything I desired to be. I sensed if I could see divine qualities in others then perhaps I could develop them in myself. England and Dartington became an opportunity for me to be Dorothy Elmhirst. An ordinary woman involved in a rural re-generation project with her husband.

BIOGRAPHER

I have a sense from Tagore he believed we should all search for a balance between an inner reflective life and outer worldly activity. And that God is that balancing power within us.

DOROTHY

So you are interested in spirituality?

BIOGRAPHER

I'm interested in history and psychology.

DOROTHY

So you see spirituality in terms of history and psychology?

BIOGRAPHER

In a way.

DOROTHY

But does not the spirit create the ideas of history and psychology? That spiritual knowledge is developing a relationship with the natural world as it should be. In losing our spirituality, we lose our connection to the world, to our selves. Shakespeare understood this:

This is no flattery: these are counsellors
That feelingly persuade me what I am.
Sweet are the uses of adversity,
Which like the toad, ugly and venomous,
Wears yet a precious jewel in his head;
And this our life exempt from public haunt,
Finds tongues in trees, books in the running brooks,

Sermons in stones, and good in every thing.
I would not change it.
Duke Senior's speech from Shakespeare's As You Like It.

BIOGRAPHER
So Dartington became your Forest of Arden.

DOROTHY
Shakespeare has been one of the greatest teachers in my life.
Shakespeare, and of course Mischa – their work always reaching out
beyond the material world, drawing back a veil to a realm beyond.

BIOGRAPHER
A realm beyond? You really are committed to a spirit world?
Dorothy takes a moment. She is not denying his assertion, but focuses on
the idea of her 'commitment'.

DOROTHY
My commitment is to education and truth, but both must embrace the
spirit.

BIOGRAPHER
Hence the Dartington school – a place to set children's spirits and minds
free.

DOROTHY
Our original prospectus stated: 'This school is for adventure.' It was the
key to everything that followed.
Dorothy looks to the horizon squinting. The Biographer tries to see what
she's looking at.
There he goes! A true man of nature in search of the elusive warbler. I do
hope history will remember Leonard and his vision. The English are so
rarely kind to their own. They tend to romanticise all others, except
perhaps Americans.

75

BIOGRAPHER

After the school was formed you had two children, Ruth and William.

DOROTHY

I found it all quite a strain without a proper home. Leonard was busy with the Dartington renovations and I was forty two when my youngest, Bill was born. Leonard would say, 'No spring chicken'. I was not a perfect mother, a little depressed at times perhaps. I see that now. I was also rather absent on many occasions – Who's looking after Lily?

BIOGRAPHER

I'd prefer not to discuss my life.

DOROTHY

Why so closed ? You challenge me, but spend your time in shadow.

BIOGRAPHER

Cathy, my childminder, looks after Lily. She's good for her.

DOROTHY

Would it not be good for Lily to see you happy?

BIOGRAPHER

My happiness died!
Implying his deceased partner and Lily's mother.

DOROTHY

Lily needs your happiness in her life. She perhaps needs . . .
She has touched a nerve – his frustration surfaces.

BIOGRAPHER

Sorry – I'm very sorry. I can't be how you are. You look forward – incline yourself into the world, the future, rather than retreating from it as many do. As perhaps I do.

DOROTHY

The future need hold no fear. Last summer, I began to sort out letters and divided for the children the correspondence that seemed important for them to keep. Letters bring back so vividly certain memories, but I feel their ownership is really the senders, not the receivers. I am returning many of them to their owners.

BIOGRAPHER

Why now?

DOROTHY

Just preparing. To leave things tidy.

BIOGRAPHER

Is that how you want things to be – tidy?

DOROTHY

One has very little control over how one is perceived by others, so it's good to be tidy.
A piece of untidiness left for him is why she allowed the Cecil Beaton photographs to be taken at all. The Biographer wants reasons for everything.

BIOGRAPHER

But I could never understand the Cecil Beaton portraits. It seems out of character for you to show yourself in that way.

DOROTHY

Oh, I think Mr Beaton perceived me as that rather odd American living in Devonshire. I was desperately self-conscious, but I think perhaps Ben Britten persuaded me to have them taken. I was an oddity for the English set, you see, so I expect was needed to complete the 'Beaton collection'.

BIOGRAPHER

Sarcasm?

DOROTHY

That's almost wit though, isn't it?

BIOGRAPHER

He did take some delightfully enigmatic photographs of you.
Dorothy strikes the pose from the Cecil Beaton shoot. The biographer plays Cecil Beaton with a camp demeanour.

Biographer as CECIL BEATON

Mrs Elmhirst you look lovely, really really lovely. Quite still now please.
Exposure made. Now perhaps without the hat.
Dorothy mimes removing the hat.
You don't enjoy having your photograph taken do you Mrs Elmhirst?

DOROTHY

Actually I do not, but if I am to be photographed, I could wish for nobody better than you: Mr Beaton.

Biographer as CECIL BEATON

Bet you say that to all the boys.
Dorothy tries not to laugh as he frames his shot.
Quite still again please Mrs Elmhirst.
Another exposure is made.
Exquisite. Now perhaps think of a place where your heart lies and imagine that for me. Yes, that's wonderful – hold that, hold that.
Dorothy gaze becomes distant. The photograph is taken.

BIOGRAPHER

Where did your heart lie Dorothy? What did you really feel for Mischa Chekhov?
Dorothy feels rather ambushed by the question. Mischa Chekhov was the nephew of the playwright Anton Chekhov, but has become regarded as one of the greatest actors and acting theoreticians of the twentieth century. He formed the Chekhov Theatre Studio at Dartington in 1936, but it was forced to close because of the war threat in 1938 when the Chekhov Theatre Studio re-located to America.

DOROTHY

Well, when Beatrice confirmed she wanted to train as an actor – we thought –

BIOGRAPHER

What a tragedy! Look I know all about her finding Chekhov in New York and bringing him to Dartington, but Dorothy you fell in love with him!

DOROTHY

Beatrice encouraged me to join the training – I became enthralled by the work.

BIOGRAPHER

Enthralled.

DOROTHY

Please, I do hope we're not going to argue over this.

BIOGRAPHER

In your Chekhov journal it says Mischa thought your performance so weak during a rehearsal that you cried for the whole day.

DOROTHY

I felt lost, quite devastated. Nobody had ever challenged me like that. I asked where the weakness lay? Was in my will, my depth of feelings or my imagination? Chekhov said 'in none of these regions. But that a weakness lies in outward expression and that a fear seems to get hold of me.' That thought made me very sad.

BIOGRAPHER

But he said 'fear'?

DOROTHY

It was part of the training to open up – to understand ourselves and go beyond.

*Dorothy's daughter Beatrice Straight in an adaptation of Dostoevsky's
The Possessed in which she made her Broadway debut in 1939.*

BIOGRAPHER
You see for me it sounds as if he thought you repressed. You resisted the Beaton portraits, you repressed your feelings for Chekhov and you're reticent about having this biography done!

DOROTHY
No, I have nothing to hide.

BIOGRAPHER
Dorothy, you left Leonard, Dartington and England to be with Mischa in America for God's sake!
Dorothy feels frustrated that he cannot understand their relationship was non-sexual.
Your rehearsal notebook from the Dostoevsky production of 'The Possessed' suggests –

DOROTHY
How have you come by these things?

BIOGRAPHER
Just listen. '13th June 1938. Scene with Nicholas. Found difficulty with line: *'Now I know you love me.'* Mischa asked me to say it to him, quite simply and directly, and then it seemed to come more easily.'
Speaks with a strong Russian accent.

Biographer as MICHAEL CHEKHOV
Once, my dear Dorothy. Everything you say must be very decisive, everything must be clear and warm, but never sentimental. Again – 'Now I know you love me – now I know you love me'.
Dorothy refuses to play.

DOROTHY
What are you trying to do? Yes I loved Mischa, but not in the way you understand love.

BIOGRAPHER

I understand love!

DOROTHY

I think you understand passion and need, but Mischa was capable of spiritual love.

BIOGRAPHER

Listen to me, I understand love! Every day I have a small child that reminds me of my love, a deep, deep love – a sacred love. A love that should never ever have ended – never, ever, ever!

DOROTHY

Is this how you're going to live, as a victim!

BIOGRAPHER

That's a cruel cruel thing to say.

DOROTHY

No, you wanted honesty from me. Trust it is out of love that I say this. You have become habituated to your pain. You live in fear, not me! Lily's mother is no longer here, but her spirit is all around you and Lily.

BIOGRAPHER

You never knew her and you don't know me!

DOROTHY

I see someone avoiding their deepest feelings while seeing the world through a dark glass.

BIOGRAPHER

I think it's you who are trying to hide their feelings. I think you've spent a lot of your life hiding from being the real you. Escaping from being Dorothy the Whitney heiress; Dorothy the poor widow; and then Dorothy the actress! Wasn't leaving Mischa in America just another example of you being fearful and running away!

Dorothy, top, in rehearsal with Michael Chekhov.

DOROTHY

I was needed in England!

BIOGRAPHER

Oh, duty, always duty! Wasn't there a duty to the Chekhov group and the production on Broadway?

DOROTHY

Yes, and it was a very difficult decision.

BIOGRAPHER

I don't understand you.

DOROTHY

Then at least now you're searching for truth! You must appreciate I was pulled in so many directions all my life. This was a moment, a few months, just for me – just for me. To be an actor, an artist. You can't imagine the joy I felt. I had spent most of my life supporting others, but to be an artist for just a few months. To be able to give myself up to Dostoevsky, to serve an artist like Mischa Chekhov – it was the most incredible time.

BIOGRAPHER

But why then leave the Chekhov production which had made you so happy?

DOROTHY

It became obvious that I must return to England, my home. Dartington and Leonard needed me, still need me, more than the Chekhov Theatre group needed an ordinary actress.

BIOGRAPHER

But Dorothy, Dorothy you've been so incredibly creative in everything you've ever done. Absolutely everything! Surely creativity is not reserved for the arts alone.

Dorothy is moved by his recognition.

DOROTHY

Perhaps, during the war, I turned to the Dartington garden for beauty and solace. While touching the soil and watching the plants develop, I felt connected again to the creative whole. In each plant's struggle for survival and territory I saw a mirrored image on the world's stage. Petals became national flags, decaying trees, war-torn battlegrounds. There is something about gardening . . .

BIOGRAPHER

I think – I sense it's about the joy of growth. Lily is my flower.

DOROTHY

I remember after a planting I would return each day and watch the delicate, but incessant progress. Each seedling struggling for life, labouring through soil, enduring weather. Each with its own character searching for life and light, life and light.

BIOGRAPHER

So you cultivated your garden from inner principles. Although you were active during the war years trying to galvanise support for the British by giving talks in America.

DOROTHY

What became most curious to me was how such adversity could bring such a quality of optimism and humour from the British. Everywhere you went in London you would see signs and notices written up to make you laugh. A barber's shop which had been badly destroyed put up a sign saying 'close shave'. A determined old lady put up a notice on her dilapidated shop front saying 'open as usual', and someone else put a sign next door where a shop had once stood saying 'more open than usual'.

BIOGRAPHER

My grandfather used to say 'Those who laugh most live longest'.

Dorothy digging in the Dartington Hall garden.

DOROTHY

And one knows that the spirit which can laugh at disaster, is the spirit which can never be defeated.

BIOGRAPHER

Did the war not damage your faith at all?

DOROTHY

It is a complex thing. I've often found discussions about god and spirituality sadly divide people. We live in a scientific age, where people resist things that cannot easily be proved.

BIOGRAPHER

Well of course, but where would we be without trust in evidence-based scientific facts?

DOROTHY

I think that's your most interesting question yet.
Dorothy spots Leonard walking back.
There's Jerry! I wonder if he's found his warbler.
The Biographer takes out his mobile computer phone and becomes slightly isolated by light.

BIOGRAPHER

Hello Cathy, is everything ok?
Dorothy appears smiling, as if receiving good news.

Dorothy as CATHY

Yes of course. Are you having a good day too?

BIOGRAPHER

It's been interesting.

Dorothy as CATHY

Tell me, is the research going well?

BIOGRAPHER

Quoting Hamlet.
Truly wondrous.

Dorothy as CATHY
Dorothy as Cathy encourages him to embrace ambiguity.

And therefore as a stranger give it welcome.
There are more things in heaven and earth,
Than are dreamt of in your philosophy.

BIOGRAPHER
Yes. I've realised I don't know Dorothy at all well. She is still a mystery
– all this work and still such a mystery.

Dorothy as CATHY
Have you talked to her about it?

BIOGRAPHER
Dorothy's dead.

Dorothy as CATHY
And you're going to let a little thing like that stop you. I talk to imaginary
people all the time, and so does Lily.

BIOGRAPHER
I better go. I'll see you later.
He pauses, not terminating the call.

Dorothy as CATHY
Is there something else you wanted to ask?

BIOGRAPHER
I wondered whether we might have dinner one night?

Dorothy as CATHY

That would be nice.

BIOGRAPHER

Ok then.

Lights flood through to create a new beginning. Biographer enters, transforming as if to the real Leonard in the time of Dorothy's 1959 memoir. Perhaps he puts on a jacket or glasses to prompt the actuality of the transformation to Leonard Elmhirst, to identify that this scene is not a scene with the Biographer, even though played by the same actor.

LEONARD

I've bought you a cordial. Are you still musing on the memoir?

DOROTHY

Jerry, I was imagining a biography about me.

LEONARD

Sounds a splendid idea, quite splendid. People should know about you.

DOROTHY

And you too, dear. We've done a good thing creating Dartington, haven't we?

LEONARD

Of course we have. We've proved there can be other ways to do things.

DOROTHY

I've had a wonderful life Jerry.

LEONARD

You're making it sound like it's over. Bill's in a feisty mood today. He's having a wonderfully heated discussion with Mike about Joseph Conrad.

Leonard and Dorothy, Pink Sands, Harbour Island, Bahamas.

DOROTHY

Are they arguing in earnest?

LEONARD

Dearest, Mike and Bill are on different sides of the trenches. Bill's Bill –
sees the divine working in ways Mike will never understand. Perhaps Bill
will become the most radical of us all?

DOROTHY

Yes.

LEONARD

Mike's so deeply political. The world moves under the influence of
people and ideas. They will never see things the same way.

DOROTHY

No. I was just thinking about the garden.

LEONARD

The Dartington garden?

DOROTHY

Yes, I wanted to say I realised how it is the shadows which add so much
to the beauty and depth of everything. Now that the beech leaves are out,
the trees are beginning to cast shadows, and it gives immediately a kind
of variety and subtlety and mystery to the whole scene. There are always
shadows, you see.
A quiet moment. Leonard transforms to the Biographer.

BIOGRAPHER

Dorothy, this is 1959 for you, but for me . . . I'm looking back at your
life.

DOROTHY

So you know things that are still to happen . . . to me, to the family, to
Dartington?

Dorothy dealing with correspondence, Dartington Hall.

BIOGRAPHER

Yes.

DOROTHY

You know when I'll die?
Biographer is reluctant to answer.
You do know when I die. It's all right. My heart attacks four years ago
have encouraged me to prepare. That's why I'm doing this really . . .
sorting out the letters and writing the memoir . . . while I can.

BIOGRAPHER

Yes, of course.

DOROTHY

Will I have time to sort out everything?

BIOGRAPHER

Yes, pretty much.

DOROTHY

That's a weight off my mind. Thank you. And the children – they're all well?

BIOGRAPHER

They all survive you.

DOROTHY

Such a joy to know that I brought life into the world, and with
grandchildren, too.

BIOGRAPHER

Your legacy reaches far beyond these shores in infinite ways.

DOROTHY

Sounds very spiritual to me.
They smile.
Shall I read you the start of my memoir.

BIOGRAPHER

That would be nice.

DOROTHY

I rose this morning with the dawn. And watched the slow suffusion of the light restore to earth the pattern of the whole. And in the sky, though clouds obscured the sun, I knew that he was there far, far above. A great cloud caught the flame and carried high the glow from far beneath.

BIOGRAPHER

I feel we should leave something.

DOROTHY

The only thing we can leave is our selves, and our truest selves are the most honourable remains of all. Shakespeare said, 'No legacy is so rich as honesty'.
Dorothy quoting All's Well that Ends Well.
This ground will endure, and my hope that this garden be my enduring epitaph. Words are of no matter.

BIOGRAPHER

This nothing's more than matter.
This line from Laertes in Hamlet cues Dorothy to remember Ophelia's speeches as she looks around her.

DOROTHY

There's rosemary, that's for remembrance – pray you, love, remember. And there is pansies, that's for thoughts.
Dorothy sees her resting ground – an area in the Dartington garden. The biographer picks up her diary.

BIOGRAPHER

Dorothy lived the last year of her life as she'd always done: searching, learning, supporting and caring. Her last week, December 1968, shows a full diary as always. It starts with a late addition to her pre-arranged appointments. Monday 9th 'Anthony died'. Perhaps she thought it might be a good week to die herself and join her young grandson.

Tuesday 10th College ends – Jerry London – 2nd year college dance at 2:30pm.

Wednesday 11th, Dorcas at 11am, evening – folk songs.

Thursday 12th at 12pm, Mrs Miller dress fitting.

A friend saw Dorothy near Totnes that morning. It was a freezing December day, 'You do look cold' Dorothy said, apparently frozen herself.

Friday 13th. A trustee meeting scheduled. Dorothy, looking grey, takes to her bed.

Saturday 14th December. Dorothy still unwell, but still heard laughing. Laughing at death? That evening she wishes Leonard, her son Bill and Michael Young farewell, as they attend the school's Christmas party. Jerry returns early.

Biographer moves towards Dorothy.

He sits at her bedside as she passes away just before Bill and Michael return at 10:45pm.

Michael Tippett Spiritual: 'Steal Away' from 'Child of Our Time' – audio fades to low level.

DOROTHY

This is the way I thought God shows himself to us – never directly, since the fire would be too great, but through reflection of this light in human souls and in the whole creation of his world.

ENDS